Deborah

Storyline **Verlie Ward**
Illustrations **Steven Butler**

Deborah lived with her husband in the hills near Bethel. Deborah was a judge, the only woman judge at that time. When people did not agree, they would come to Deborah for help. She would help them solve their problems.

Because she was wise and good, God chose Deborah to lead the people of Israel back to him.

One day God spoke to Deborah. God told her that he would destroy Israel's enemies, the wicked men who ruled over them.

So Deborah called on a man named Barak. "God wants you to gather men for an army," Deborah told Barak. "You are to choose ten thousand men and go to Mount Tabor to fight King Jabin."

Barak was very afraid. He knew that King Jabin's soldiers were experienced fighters, but the men of Israel were mostly shepherds and farmers. He knew that Jabin's army had strong weapons and hundreds of chariots, but Israel had none.

So Barak said, "I will go, but only if you come with me."

Deborah said, "If I go, the people will say this battle was won by a woman."

But Barak didn't care. He was willing to do anything so Deborah would go with him.

Soon Barak had gathered ten thousand men. They marched with Deborah and Barak to the top of Mount Tabor and set up camp.

When King Jabin heard that Deborah and the men of Israel were camped on Mount Tabor, he was very angry. He called his army and got ready for war.

He gathered thousands of armed soldiers and hundreds of chariots in the valley below. They were ready to fight.

But Deborah and the men of Israel were not ready to fight. They waited on the mountain while Deborah listened to God. She was waiting for God to tell her when the time was right.

Then Deborah said, "Now is the time for action! God is leading us. He has delivered the enemy into our hands."

Barak looked down at the enemy army. He looked at its weapons and chariots. He did not see how Israel could win.

But Barak trusted Deborah. Giving a mighty shout, he led his men down the mountain toward the army below.

Suddenly huge, black clouds covered the sky. The thunder crashed and the lightening flashed. A heavy, blinding rain poured down. The horses screamed and the chariots became stuck in the mud. The enemy soldiers became frightened and confused.

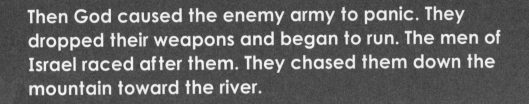

Then God caused the enemy army to panic. They
dropped their weapons and began to run. The men of
Israel raced after them. They chased them down the
mountain toward the river.

And there the raging flood waters swept the entire
enemy army away!

Deborah and the men of Israel returned from battle. As they marched, they sang songs of praise to God. The people from the villages gathered for a great celebration. They thanked God who had delivered them from their enemies.

After this battle, the people of Israel began to serve God faithfully once again.

And there was peace in the land for forty years.